THE PADRE ON HORSEBACK

A sketch of
EUSEBIO FRANCISCO KINO • S.J.
Apostle to the Pimas

by

Herbert Eugene Bolton

LOYOLA UNIVERSITY PRESS, CHICAGO
1986

CONTENTS

PREFACE

FOREWORD

MULTUM IN PARVO

THE MISSIONARIES

EUSEBIO FRANCISCO KINO

SPLENDID WAYFARING

STUBBORN CALIFORNIA

LA PAZ

SAN BRUNO

CALIFORNIA IN THE BALANCE

PIMA LAND

DOLORES

MISSION BUILDING

TRAIL MAKING

THE BLUE SHELLS

CATTLE KING

PROTECTOR OF THE BORDER

HARD RIDING

STRONG OF HEART

VELARDE'S EULOGY

FOREWORD

IN THE SECOND HALF of the nineteenth century one of the greatest of American historians (some will use the superlative without qualification), Francis Parkman, opened a new vista to the students of American colonial history when he went beyond the narrow limits of the Atlantic seaboard strip to uncover for them the American world which the French had made and which the English coveted early and ultimately won. Parkman was dead not quite a decade when his pioneering spirit came alive in another man who did for another area of North America and for another colonial people what the great New Englander had done for the French. In the summer of 1902 Herbert Eugene Bolton left Austin and headed for Mexico.

The new history instructor at the University of Texas, transplanted the previous September from his native Wisconsin, had had his curiosity awakened by the Spaniards in the few short months in the state where he was putting his recently won doctor's degree to work. All around him these other American colonizers had left their mark. One could hardly tell the Texas story by beginning with Stephen Austin or Sam Houston or their fellows—it could be *a* Texas history, but hardly *the* Texas history. And in that day little had been done on those early chapters of *the* story. So off to Mexico went Doctor Bolton in an attempt to find the pieces.

It did not take many summers to show Bolton that the story of Spain in America was a vast field of history crying for attention and sympathetic scholarly understanding. Parkman had written of a French frontier and, in so doing, had broadened the American historian's vision. Bolton's professor at the University of Wisconsin, dynamic Frederick Jackson Turner, had been pushing the study of another frontier in the days when Bolton was listening to him as an undergraduate. Now here was a Spanish frontier in American history, the borderlands. This Bolton set himself to interpret.

Bolton had almost become a lawyer, for as an undergraduate his ambitions originally ran in that direction. But several of his Wisconsin professors had left a deep mark on him, notably Turner and another historian, this time a medievalist, Charles Homer Haskins. In 1896 he had returned to his university as a graduate student and assistant to Turner. Next, he went on to the University of Pennsylvania, as a Harrison fellow, to earn his Ph.D. under the direction of John Bach McMaster. Awarded the doctorate in 1899, he returned to his native Wisconsin and for two years taught at Milwaukee State Normal School.

THE PADRE ON HORSEBACK

In 1901 Bolton had joined the Department of History at the University of Texas.

The summer of 1902 opened a half-century of some of the most productive historical scholarship in the record of American history writing. The cerebral hemorrhage which struck down the great man and ultimately took him to his grave on January 30, 1953, came in July of 1952, just a few days short of the eighty-second anniversary of his birth (1870) and a few days after the golden anniversary of his first venture into the archives of Mexico.

He was hardly back from his summer excursion when he began to share his vision with the scholarly world. The October 1902 number of the Texas State Historical Association *Quarterly* carried an article of his, "Some Materials for Southwestern History in the Archivo General de México." Others followed in the next years, as Bolton continued his summer forays and put his findings on the history of Spanish Texas into print. During these years, too, he made important contributions on the Texas tribes to Frederick Webb Hodge's *Handbook of American Indians North of Mexico,* having found much new and valuable materials concerning them in the almost forgotten, and certainly neglected, papers of the first white men to know them, the Spaniards. In 1907 Bolton went off to Mexico,

THE PADRE ON HORSEBACK

this time to spend the whole year in surveying and cataloguing the data which introduced American historians to the wealth of American history to be found in the dust-covered *legajos* of the Mexican depositories. In those days in Mexico a pair of coveralls was as necessary a part of the scholar's baggage as was pencil and paper. The *Guide to Materials for the History of the United States in the Principal Archives of Mexico* appeared in 1913, to take its place beside similar volumes, which with the sponsorship of the Carnegie Foundation of Washington and under the general editorship of J. Franklin Jameson were bringing like materials from other foreign archives to the notice of American historians. Bolton's work definitely established him as a leading scholar in the field of things Hispanic as they touched United States history.

Between his year in the Mexican archives and the publication of the *Guide* much had happened to Bolton. In 1909 Stanford University lured him away from Texas and made him its professor of American history—his departure left an admiring and enthusiastic Texas following much distressed and occasioned sharp criticism of their state university for allowing this bit of academic "piracy." Two years later, shrewd and perceptive Henry Morse Stephens, who was expanding the Department of History at the University of Cal-

THE PADRE ON HORSEBACK

ifornia, outbid Stanford and brought Bolton to Berkeley. In 1910 Stephens, who saw the day of America history dawning, had tried to sign Frederick Jackson Turner for his department. But Harvard had discovered the frontier and offered Turner a chair. Stephens, with little hesitation, then turned to Bolton whom he had found as a frequent visitor to the recently acquired collections of Hubert Howe Bancroft and whom he came to recognize as the ideal man to mine that treasure trove of Western history.

The University of California at Berkeley was Bolton's home base for the rest of his scholarly life, forty years plus. In 1916 he was named acting curator of the Bancroft Library. In 1919, on the death of Henry Morse Stephens, he became chairman of the Department of History and began to build it into one of the foremost in the United States. Bolton was a fine academic administrator; but he was even greater as a teacher, a research director, and a productive scholar.

During his four decades at California he trained and inspired over a hundred Ph.D.'s and several times that number of Masters. His "boys" and "girls" went forth to broaden the knowledge of American history so that it might properly include the Spaniards among its important makers.

The list of Bolton's works, started with the *Guide*

THE PADRE ON HORSEBACK

in 1913, grew longer year by year, most of them bringing the Spanish borderlands into focus. There was *Athanase de Mézières and the Louisiana-Texas Frontier*, in 1914; *Texas in the Middle Eighteenth Century*, in 1915; *Spanish Exploration in the Southwest, 1542-1706*, in 1916; *Kino's Historical Memoir of Pimerá Alta*, in 1919; *The Spanish Borderlands*, in 1921; *Arredondo's Historical Proof of Spain's Title to Georgia*, in 1925; *The Debatable Land, a Sketch of the Anglo-Spanish Contest for the Georgia Country* (with Mary Ross), also in 1925. The next year saw the first of his volumes of the history of California; these revived some of the important sources, made available in translation and critical editions for the first time. There was Paloú, Crespi, Font, and Anza; and this California group was climaxed in 1931 by *Outpost of Empire: The Story of the Founding of San Francisco*, a work which was awarded the gold medal of the Commonwealth Club of California. In 1932 Bolton came out with the charming little work which is being brought back into circulation with this reprint edition, *The Padre on Horseback;* in 1936 he followed it with a fuller biography of his favorite Black Robe, *Rim of Christendom: A Biography of Eusebio Francisco Kino, Pacific Coast Pioneer*. Four of his shorter studies, including his presidential address to the American Historical Association in 1932, were gathered into the

THE PADRE ON HORSEBACK

little volume *Wider Horizons of American History,* appearing in 1939. There was still a gap in his own borderland coverage; he sought to fill this in his last two major works, *Coronado, Knight of Pueblos and Plains,* in 1949, and *Pageant in the Wilderness, The Story of the Escalante Expedition to the Interior Basin,* in 1950. The years were not given him to tell the story of Padre Juan María Salvatierra, Jesuit founder of the Baja California enterprise, for whose biography he had long been gathering materials.

In his role as teacher he produced two influential texts to implement his two favorite undergraduate courses—*The Colonization of North America, 1492-1783* (with Thomas Maitland Marshall, one of his early graduate students), on 1920, and *History of the Americas: A Syllabus with Maps,* in 1928. The first shocked the editorial readers to whom the publisher submitted the manuscript—the proposed book was so ill proportioned and strangely conceived that better than a quarter of it was gone before the English made the "first American foundation" at Jamestown in 1607. It would take American historians a long time to recognize that 1607 was an important but not an opening date in the story—Bolton and his "boys" were going to right the balance in favor of truer American perspective. *History of the Americas* put between hard covers the concept of American history which Bolton had been popularizing on the California campus for ten or more years before 1928. He had been trying to show his listeners that the Anglo experience was only a part of the larger New World story, in which Spaniards figured prominently, along with the French and the Portuguese, the Dutch and the Swedes, and even the Russians. Even after the achievement of independence American experience, Anglo and Latin, had much in common, along with the many obvious differences.

REPRINTED herewith is a delightful short study, a masterful sketch of the career of the great Jesuit missioner of the Southwestern Borderlands, Eusebio Francisco Kino; and it shows Bolton well. Kino was an excellent laboratory specimen, so to speak, to prove the validity of the theory which Bolton had so brilliantly voiced in his penetrating essay of 1917, "The Mission as a Frontier Institution in the Spanish American Colonies." Further, it is a neat segment in that fuller borderlands story which Bolton, as he often said himself, sought to "parkmanize."

This little work can introduce the reader to a great American historian, as well as to a very American part of the larger American epic. Bolton was a man who

THE PADRE ON HORSEBACK

before the days of the Good Neighbor Policy and the *Alianza para Progreso* knew that a knowledge of our fellow Americans in their historical development must precede understanding and be basic to fostering those traits which will make us *simpáticos*. The scholar who already knows and appreciates Bolton will be happy to add this little work to his library.

Parkman broadened our historical horizons to include the French; Turner helped us to place the Mississippi Valley in correct perspective; Webb sought to explain the Great Plains; Bolton uncovered the Spanish frontier and put the borderlands in the true American picture—one and all, integral parts of our past and quite as vital thereto as Jamestown and Williamsburg, Plymouth and Boston.

JOHN FRANCIS BANNON, S.J.
St. Louis University
1963

PREFACE

NOTABLE among historical revivals in North America is the new interest in Father Kino, the incomparable pioneer of the Southwest and the Pacific Coast. Famed among his contemporaries and eulogized by his successors, he gradually dropped from view. Then one day his autobiography was discovered in a dusty archive. The precious manuscript, lost for a century and a half, revealed an astounding personage. Slowly, as the account was read, Kino's recreated figure rose above the historical horizon; then suddenly, and as if by a common burst of insight, his significance was grasped.

The result was what might be expected. The world is now anxious to do Kino honor. Both in Europe and America his remarkable life work is being eagerly studied. Archives have been explored, family garrets ransacked, and fabulous sums paid for the missionary's autograph letters. The Jesuits print Kino's name high in their long list of apostles to the American heathendom. Southwestern cowboys stand aghast and almost skeptical at his well authenticated feats in the saddle. Geographers spread his fame as explorer and cartographer. Italy hails him as a noble if nearly forgotten son. Germany is proud to have been the inimitable Jesuit's schoolmaster. Spain points to him as one of the most puissant builders of her colonial empire. Mexico cherishes his memory as a conspicuous pioneer of her vast and historic West Coast. California lauds him as the inspirer of Salvatierra, her first successful colonizer. Arizona reveres him as her most prodigious and exemplary pioneer.

Typical of this renaissance is the formation of the Kino Memorial Committee, devoted to the erection of a suitable monument for the great missionary of the Southwest. At the head of this laudable movement stands the energetic scholar, Frank C. Lockwood, of the University of Arizona. It is to promote the same end that this brief sketch of Kino is now published. In substance, it is what was said informally in an address delivered at the Kino Celebration held at Tucson in March, 1932. In the main it is based upon the introduction to my edition of Kino's *Favores Celestiales* published in 1919, now out of print and excessively rare.

It is my earnest hope that in due time a suitable monument to Father Eusebio may be erected. Kino's characteristic place was in the saddle; and no statue would be more appropriate for this remarkable Knight of the Cross than one representing him as the Padre on Horseback.

MULTUM IN PARVO

THE PROBLEM of the biographer of Father Kino is to tell much in little, so many and long continued were his activities. He was great not only as missionary and church builder, but also as explorer and ranchman. The occupation of California by the Jesuits was the direct result of Kino's residence there and of his persistent efforts in its behalf, for it was from Kino that Salvatierra, founder of the permanent California missions, got his inspiration for that work. By Kino or directly under his supervision missions were founded on both sides of the Sonora–Arizona boundary, on the Magdalena, Altar, Sonóita, and Santa Cruz rivers.

To Kino is due the credit for first traversing in detail and accurately mapping the whole of Pimería Alta, the name then applied to southern

Arizona and northern Sonora. Considered quantitatively alone, his work of exploration was astounding. During his twenty-four years of residence at the mission of Dolores, between 1687 and 1711, he made more than fifty journeys inland, an average of more than two per year. These journeys varied from a hundred to nearly a thousand miles in length. They were all made on horseback. In the course of them he crossed and recrossed repeatedly and at varying angles all of the two hundred miles of country between the Magdalena and the Gila and the two hundred and fifty miles between the San Pedro and the Colorado. When he first opened them nearly all his trails were either absolutely untrod by civilized man or had been altogether forgotten. They were made through country inhabited by unknown tribes who might but fortunately did not offer him personal violence, though they sometimes proved too threatening for the nerve of his companions. One of his routes was over a forbidding, waterless waste, which at a later date became the graveyard of scores of travelers who died of thirst because they lacked Father

THE PADRE ON HORSEBACK

Kino's pioneering skill. I refer to the Camino del Diablo, or Devil's Highway, from Sonóita to the Gila. In the prosecution of these journeys Kino's energy and hardihood were almost beyond belief.

All the foregoing was the work of a man of action, and it was worthy work well done. But Kino also found time to write. Historians have long known and had access to a diary, three "relations," two or three letters, and a famous map, all by Kino, and all important for the history of the region where he worked. His map published in 1705 was the first of Pimería based on actual exploration, and for more than a hundred years was the principal map of the region in existence. And there has recently come to light in the archives of Mexico a vastly more important work—a complete history, written by Kino himself at his little mission of Dolores, covering nearly his whole career in America. It was known to and used by the early Jesuit historians, and then lay forgotten till the twentieth century. It is now found to be the source of practically all that has been known of the work of Kino and his companions, and to contain much that never has been known before. Kino, therefore, was not only the first great missionary, ranchman, explorer, and geographer of Pimería Alta, but his book was the first and will be for all time the principal history of his region during his quarter century.

THE MISSIONARIES

ONLY WITH EXTREME DIFFICULTY can we of this twentieth century age comprehend the ideal which inspired the missionary pioneers of our Southwest. We can understand why man should struggle to conquer a wilderness for the wealth which it will yield; tunnel mountains to bring forth gold from their interior; build roads of steel over, through, or under them to develop and transport their treasure; construct great irrigation works to cause the desert to bloom; or apply science to the art of agriculture in order to make two blades grow where formerly there was but one. All of these kinds of effort to exploit the wealth of an undeveloped country and make it habitable by civilized man we can understand and we approve. But almost incomprehensible to us is the sixteenth century ideal which brought to the Southwest its first pioneers of European civilization—the brown-mantled Franciscan and the black-robed Jesuit missionaries.

The medieval world was energized by the Christian Church, whose central aim was the salvation of souls. At the opening of the modern era the expansion of the geographical horizon of Europe, through the great voyages of discovery, revealed to Christendom millions of human beings without the means of salvation according to the Christian plan; and it was but logical that the Church should assume the responsibility of furnishing the means of saving these millions from involuntary perdition.

The chief means provided was the Christian mission to heathen lands. Paul and his companions had set the example in the Apostolic Age. In medieval times St. Augustine imitated that example in Britain, St. Patrick in Ireland, St. Columban in France, and St. Boniface in Germany. In this period missionary effort was directed largely through the great Order of St. Benedict. The expanding opportunity for missionary work after the

THE PADRE ON HORSEBACK

discovery of America promoted the founding of new orders and the development of the older ones. Prominent among those which took part in the conversion of the New World were the Franciscans, the Dominicans, and the Jesuits.

Step by step through the sixteenth, seventeenth, and eighteenth centuries the heathen tribes of North America were brought by them under the influence of Christianity and into contact with European civilization. In Spain's domain Franciscans, Dominicans, and Jesuits labored side by side in the Great Valley and on the central plateau of Mexico; Franciscans converted the natives of Florida, New Mexico, and Texas; the Jesuits were the pioneers of Sinaloa, Sonora, Arizona, and Lower California. After their expulsion in the middle eighteenth century, their places were taken by Franciscans and Dominicans. The Franciscan missions of Upper California, the last outpost of Spain's vast empire, became celebrated throughout the world. In New France the Jesuits spread the Faith in Canada and the Mississippi Valley. The missionary story of North America is paralleled by a contemporary South American record of even greater scope, and equally impressive in character.

These men came inspired by zeal for the saving of souls. Many of them were sons of distinguished families, who might have occupied positions of honor and distinction in Europe; most of them were men of liberal education; nearly all of them were zealous for the Faith, and wholly uninterested in private gain. Yet the country where they worked is now full of deluded men who are looking for the lost and hidden treasure of the missionaries of olden time. Vain task! for the true soldier of the Cross was occupied in conquering the wilderness not for gold, but for the heathen souls which it would yield.

EUSEBIO FRANCISCO KINO

PEER OF ANY of these noble spirits was Eusebio Francisco Kino, Apostle to the Pimas. Eusebio Chino* was born in Segno, a tiny village near the famous city of Trent in northern Italy. The exact date of his birth has not been determined, but we know that he was baptized on the tenth of August, 1645. It is an interesting coincidence that his advent into the world was nearly contemporaneous with that of his intimate friend, fellow countryman, and co-worker, Juan María Salvatierra, the Apostle to Lower California.[1] Kino's family, still numerous at Segno, now spell their surname Chini. In his early days our missionary signed himself Chino, or, in Latin, Chinus. When he came to America he wrote his name Kino, to retain its

---
*Pronounced Keeno.

Italian pronunciation. Spaniards sometimes wrote it Quino.[2]

Kino's cognomen was a troublesome one. In Spain Chino was the word for Chinamen: in Mexico it was also the name applied to certain mixed-bloods of low caste. Hence Father Chino changed his name to Kino. But this did not end the trouble. Kino is pronounced the same as Keno, the well-known gambling game, today popular on transatlantic ocean liners. And now Kino is the German word for cinematograph, or "movie." Hence the recent appeal from Italy by a member of the missionary's family that I write the name Chini, "because Kino smacks too much of Hollywood." But the missionary himself determined the spelling of his name in America, and I shall respect his preference.

In point of nationality Kino was typical of a large number of the early Jesuit missionaries in Sonora, Arizona, and California. That is, although he was in the service of Spain he was non-Spanish by blood and breeding. Among Kino's companions and successors, for example, we find Salvatierra, Picolo,

Minutili, and Ripaldini, bearing in their names the marks of their Italian extraction; Steiger, Keler, Sedelmayr, and Grashofer, whose names disclose their German origin; and Januske and Hostinski, whose surnames stamp them as Bohemians.

Had he chosen to do so, Kino might have enjoyed scholarly reputation, and perhaps even won fame in Europe, for during his student career at Freiburg and Ingolstadt he greatly distinguished himself in mathematics. When the Duke of Bavaria and his father, the Elector, went in 1676 from the electoral court at Munich to Ingolstadt, they engaged Kino in a discussion of mathematical sciences, with the result that the young Jesuit was offered a professorship in the University of Ingolstadt. But he preferred to become a missionary to heathen lands. To this calling he was inclined by family tradition, for he was a relative of Father Martini, famous missionary in the East and author of many works on China.

Kino's decision to become a missionary was made when he was eighteen, as the result of a serious illness. In his *Favores Celestiales* he tells us that "To the most glorious and most pious thaumaturgus and Apostle of the Indies, San Francisco Xavier, we all owe very much. I owe him, first, my life, of which I was caused to despair by the physicians in the city of Hala, of Tirol, in the year 1663; second, my entry into the Company of Jesus*; and, third, my coming to these missions." Another mark of Kino's gratitude for his recovery was the addition of Francisco to his name.³

---

*This took place two years later, in 1665, when he was twenty.

SPLENDID WAYFARING

KINO HAD HOPED to go to the Orient, literally to follow in the footsteps of his patron, but there came a call for missionaries in New Spain, and thither he was sent instead. From his Jesuit college in Bavaria he set forth in April, 1678. On June twelfth he and eighteen companions sailed from Genoa for Spain, thence to embark for Mexico. Early in the voyage they experienced a heavy storm, and later were becalmed for several days. On the way they passed numerous vessels, and as each one hove in sight they prepared to give it battle, but all proved to be friendly. Alicante was reached on the twenty-fifth of June. Thence the companions went to Cádiz, where they arrived too late to take passage in the fleet sailing to the West Indies. So they were sent up to Seville to await an opportunity to sail.[4]

Their experiences before they finally reached America were typical of missionary adventure, or of what Ortega called *Apostólicos Afanes*.

Father Gerstl, one of Kino's companions, gives a very graphic account of some phases of Seville life at this time. He was especially interested in the monopoly of industry and commerce by the Dutch and the French, of the latter of whom forty thousand lived in Seville; in the amazing numbers of clergy and monastic houses there; in the prevalence of poverty and the multitude of beggars, of whom the archbishop regularly fed twenty-two thousand out of his income; in the crude skill of the blood-letters, at whose hands one of the nineteen, Father Fischer, succumbed; in the depreciation of silver on the arrival of a treasure fleet from America; in the crude methods of public execution, and the premature burials; and in the bull fights, in which the nobles participated and on which the Church frowned.

The delay in Spain was unexpectedly long. Some royal ships sailed for America, but as they went by the African coast to get slaves the Jesuits did not embark. Private vessels also sailed, but their charge for the passage was higher than the Father Procurator was willing to pay, consequently the Jesuits awaited the departure of the next royal fleet for the West Indies.

Late in March Kino and his companions returned to Cádiz, and on the eleventh of July the West Indian fleet sailed, convoyed by two armed galleons. But the vessel on which the Jesuits embarked foundered on a rock shortly after sailing, and they returned the same night on a small boat to Cádiz. The Father Procurator now bent every energy to get passage on the other vessels, and hurried back and forth between the port authorities and the admiral of the departing fleet. About two o'clock next morning the sleeping band of Jesuits were awakened by the Procurator, put on board a boat, and taken to the fleet, already outside the harbor. The first vessel overhauled consented to take Fathers Calvanese and Borgia; the second refused to take any; on the third embarked Fathers Tilpe and Mancker; on the fourth Father Borango and Father Zarzosa, superior of the mission; on the fifth

Fathers de Angelis and Ratkay; on the sixth Fathers Strobach and Neuman. Brother Poruhradiski, who had remained on the wrecked vessel with the Jesuits' baggage, also managed to find passage on the same ship with the superior. But twelve were left behind, among them being Gerstl and Kino.[5] It was a hard blow.

Father Gerstl and seven companions now returned to Seville to wait, and to minister during an epidemic. Kino remained at Cádiz, where he observed the great comet which was visible there between December and February. The Father Procurator conducted a lawsuit to recover six thousand dollars paid in advance for passage in the wrecked vessel. Meanwhile Kino carried on a correspondence with the Duchess of Aveiro y Arcos, a patroness of missions in the Orient. Little did the young Jesuit dream that one day in the twentieth century these letters to a lady whom he had never seen would be sold to an American library at the rate of $235 a page. I have heard of a higher price being paid for letters to a lady, but not for letters by a missionary.

THE PADRE ON HORSEBACK

In January, 1681, Father Gerstl and his companions rejoined Kino at Cádiz. On the twenty-ninth they at last set sail for America. In the West Indies the fleet divided, according to custom, and eight of the eighteen companions went to New Granada, the rest continuing to Vera Cruz, which they reached on May third, after a rough voyage of over ninety days.[6]

The band of devoted Jesuits who had set out from Genoa together were destined to scatter to the ends of the earth. The story of their personal experiences in America and the islands of the western seas occupies large space in the pages of Stöcklein's *Neue Welt-Bott*. Their travels over the face of the globe take rank with the wanderings of Ulysses.

As has been stated, eight of the splendid wayfarers were sent to New Granada. Ten came to Mexico, whence some went to the Orient. Fathers Borango, Tilpe, Strobach, de Angelis, and Cuculinus went to work among the heathen of the Marianas Islands. Mancker and Klein went to the Philippines and Gerstl to China. Ratkay worked in Sonora, Neuman in Nueva Vizcaya, Kino in

California, Sonora, and Arizona. Of the four who went to Marianas Islands, three—Borango, Strobach, and De Angelis—won the martyr's crown.[7]

Father Kino's mathematical knowledge brought him into prominence as soon as he arrived in Mexico, where he at once entered into a public discussion concerning the recent comet. One of the fruits of this episode was a pamphlet published by Kino in Mexico in 1681 under the title: "Astronomical explanation of the comet which was seen all over the world during the months of November and December, 1680, and in January and February in this year of 1681, and which was observed in the City of Cádiz by Father Francisco Kino, of the Company of Jesus."[8] This little book is still one of the important historical sources of information regarding the movements of that notable comet.

STUBBORN CALIFORNIA

FATHER KINO's first missionary field in America was Lower California. For two centuries and a half the Spaniards had made weak attempts to subdue and colonize that forbidding land. California had been discovered by one of Cortés's sailors in 1533. Two years later the great conquistador himself led a colony to the Peninsula, then thought to be an island and called Santa Cruz. The enterprise failed, but Cortés continued his explorations, and Ulloa, sent out by him in 1539, rounded the cape and proved Santa Cruz to be a peninsula. Henceforth it was called California. Three years later Cabrillo, in quest of the Strait of Anian, that is, the northern passage to the Atlantic in which everybody believed, explored the outer coast of California beyond Cape Mendocino.

THE PADRE ON HORSEBACK

New interest in California followed the conquest of the Philippines by Legazpi (1565-1571); indeed, in the later sixteenth century California was as much an appendage of Manila as of Mexico. Legazpi's men discovered a practicable return route to America, down the California coast, and thereupon trade, conducted in the Manila Galleon, was established between the Philippines and Acapulco. But the voyage was long, scurvy exacted heavy tribute of crews and passengers, and a port of call was sorely needed. English pirates, too, like Drake and Cavendish, infested the Pacific, and were followed by the Dutch freebooters, known as Pichilingues. California, therefore, must be explored, protected, and peopled.

It was with these needs in view that Cermeño made his disastrous voyage down the California coast; that Vizcaíno attempted the settlement of La Paz and explored the outer shore; and that the king ordered a settlement made at Monterey.

The Monterey project failed, but settlements and missions crept up the Sinaloa and Sonora mainland, and the pearl fisheries of California attracted attention, hence new attempts were made on the Peninsula. Having little cash to spare, the monarchs tried to make pearl fishing rights pay the cost of settlement and defence. In the course of the seventeenth century, therefore, numerous contracts were made with private adventurers. By the terms the patentees agreed to people California in return for a monopoly of pearl gathering. With nearly every expedition went missionaries, to convert and help tame the heathen. In pursuance of these agreements several attempts were made to settle, especially at La Paz, where Cortés and Vizcaíno both had failed. Other expeditions were fitted out at royal expense. The names of Carbonel, Córdova, Ortega, Porter y Casante, Piñadero, and Lucenilla all stand for seventeenth century failures to colonize California.

At first the natives of the Peninsula had been docile, but they were enslaved and misused by the pearl hunters, against the royal will, and so became suspicious and hostile, as later pioneers learned. Through various misunderstandings and incomplete explorations, in the course of the century California had again come to be regarded and shown on maps as an island.

In spite of the repeated failures, another attempt at settlement was decided upon. By an agreement of December, 1678, the enterprise was entrusted to Don Isidro Atondo y Antillón. This was to be primarily a missionary venture, and the costs were to be borne by the crown. Don Isidro was given the resounding title of Governor of Sinaloa and Admiral of the Kingdom of the Californias. The spiritual ministry was assigned to the Jesuits.[9] Prophets now heralded a better day for the land of pearls.

LA PAZ

IN THE MIDST of Atondo's preparations Father Kino arrived in Mexico, and was named, with Father Matías Goñi, missionary to California. Again Kino's mathematical learning was given recognition, for the viceroy made him royal cosmographer—that is, astronomer, surveyor, and map maker—of the expedition. Before leaving Mexico, Kino prepared himself for his scientific task by studying California geography, borrowing maps for the purpose from the viceroy's palace and taking them to the Colegio Máximo de San Pedro y San Pablo to copy.[10]

It was expected that the expedition would sail in the fall of 1681, and before the end of the year Kino left the capital for his new field of labor. On November 15, while on his way through Guadalajara, he was made vicar of the Bishop of Nueva Galicia for California. As the vessels for the expedition were being built by Atondo at Pueblo de Nío, on the Sinaloa River, thither Kino made his way,[11] and there we find him in March, 1682.

Kino now became involved, innocently, in a dispute over ecclesiastical jurisdiction in California between the bishops of Guadalajara and Durango.[12] Having already a commission as vicar of the former, because of the dispute, it would seem, he applied for and obtained a similar commission from the latter.[13] This may or may not be the reason why Father Antonio Suárez was now made superior of the California mission, but so he was. Incident to the contest, Father Kino was ordered by the Bishop of Guadalajara to relinquish his commission from the rival bishop, and the question was terminated by the viceroy in favor of Guadalajara. By December fifth the vessels had left Sinaloa and were at Chacala, taking on supplies, and Fathers Suárez, Kino, and Goñi were there ready to embark. Father Suárez did not go to California, however, and Kino became superior after all.[14]

THE PADRE ON HORSEBACK

At last, on January seventeenth, 1683, the expedition sailed. The voyage was difficult, the crew was raw, and the vessels were driven into the harbor at Mazatlán. Two months after embarking they entered the Sinaloa River,[15] where they took on fresh provisions. From here they once more set sail, crossed the Gulf, and reached the coast near La Paz, already the site of so many failures. During the voyage the launch was disabled and never reached port.[16]

On April first anchor was cast and a formal proclamation issued requiring good treatment of the Indians and regulating the gathering of precious metals and pearls, the two primary interests of the expedition. Next day a site was selected and a cross set up near a fine grove of palm trees and a good well of water. On the fifth all disembarked with the royal standard, a salute was fired, three *vivas* were shouted for Carlos II, and the admiral took possession for the king, calling the province Santísima Trinidad. At the same time Kino took ecclesiastical possession.[17]

A small fort was begun at once, and a log

church and huts were erected. Sending the *Concepción* to the Río Yaqui for supplies, Atondo and Kino made minor explorations. The Indians near the settlement, though shy at first, soon became friendly, and Fathers Kino and Goñi began to study their language. But this amity did not last, and by July a state of war existed. The soldiers were now panic stricken and clamored to abandon the settlement. "It is plain," says Father Venegas, that Atondo "had with him few like those courageous and hardened men who at an earlier day had subdued America." Since the *Concepción* had not returned, and supplies were consequently short, Atondo yielded, and on July fourteenth the *San José* weighed anchor, with all the Spaniards on board. The Bay of Peace had thus again become the Bay of War.

SÁN BRUNO

ATONDO now went to the Fuerte River to refit, in order to make a new attempt farther up the California coast, where more promising lands and Indians had been reported. Setting sail again, on October sixth he landed with the missionaries and men at a bay called San Bruno, a few leagues north of the present Loreto. Here a new settlement was begun; the *San José* was sent for supplies and recruits and with dispatches for the viceroy.[18] And now, in this desert land where the soil is ever thirsty and the cactus grows tall, our missionary began another chapter in his eventful career.

The routine of life at San Bruno from December 21, 1683, to May 8, 1684, can be gleaned from the detailed diary kept by Father Kino and preserved to us in the original in the archives of

Mexico.[19] It begins with an account of an exploration by Father Kino and Ensign Contreras into the Sierra Giganta, to the west. The principal occupations at the little outpost of civilization were those connected with providing food, shelter, protection, and the conversion of the natives. The docile Indians labored willingly in building the fort, the houses, and the church, and brought such supplies as the sterile land afforded.

Father Kino's diary gives us a perfect picture of a true missionary, devoted heart and soul to the one object of converting and civilizing the natives, and for whom no incident was too trivial if it contributed to his main end. He was like the artist, or the genuine scholar, much of whose labor would be unbearable drudgery to one not inspired with the zeal of a devotee.

Kino regarded the poor natives as his personal wards. He loved them with a real affection, and ever stood ready to minister to their bodily wants or to defend them against false charges or harsh treatment. He dwelt with pleasure on all evidence of friendship shown by the Indians, and recorded every indication of their intelligence. He took sincere delight in instructing them and in satisfying their childish curiosity regarding such things as the compass, the sun dial, the lens with which he started fires, and the meaning of the symbols used in his maps.

The first task of the missionary was to win the confidence of the natives, and the direct way to their hearts was through their stomachs. Whenever a visit was made to an outlying village, therefore, gifts of maize, pinole, and other eatables were carried for all natives who might be encountered. When strangers came from a distance, they, too, were given presents. Confidence having been secured, the Indians would leave their boys with the missionaries, whose house was usually crowded with them overnight. Thus was afforded a means of teaching them the Spanish language and the rudimentary uses of clothing, and to recite the prayers, sing, and perform domestic duties.

It was with the young that Kino was especially concerned, and whenever he made an excursion he was usually followed by a troop of Indian boys running by his side, trying to keep up, or crying if left behind. Often one or more urchins might be seen triumphantly mounted behind the Father on the haunches of his horse. Kino tells with zest how a young boy who was living at the mission resisted the efforts of his parents to take him away, calling for help on "Padre Eusebio."

Nothing gave Father Kino such true pleasure as some sign that an Indian was becoming interested in the Faith.[20] He dwells at length and with evident delight on the story of a little native girl who knelt before a picture of the Virgin and begged permission to hold the Christ Child; on the progress made by his charges in repeating the prayers, singing the Salve, and reciting the Litanies; and on their zeal in helping to decorate the crude church for the celebration of the feast days.

Sometimes, as was true of all missionaries among the heathen, his ingenuity was put to the test to explain Christian concepts in the simple Indian language. A classic example is his amusing story of how he explained the Resurrection by reviving some apparently lifeless flies. When the astonished

Indians shouted *Ibimu huegite*, they gave the Father the native term which he had been seeking.

On August tenth the *San José* at last returned, bringing twenty additional soldiers, supplies, and dispatches from the viceroy. At this time Father Juan Bautista Copart also came, and on August fifteenth Father Kino made final profession within the Jesuit Order in Father Copart's hands. An extended exploration across the mountains was now projected, and during the autumn the *San José* plied to and from the Yaqui River, bringing horses, mules, and supplies. On the first voyage, made between August twenty-ninth and September twenty-fifth, Father Kino accompanied Captain Andrés, and obtained aid from the mainland missions, particularly from Father Cervantes at Torín. Bancroft conjectures that Kino "probably remained in Sonora a year," but such was by no means the case.[21] On a subsequent trip Kino's place was taken by Father Goñi. While the *San José* was making her supply voyages a new post and mission were established a few leagues inland from San Bruno at the fine wells of San Isidro.

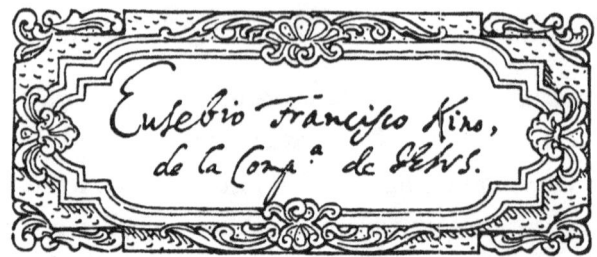

CALIFORNIA IN THE BALANCE

THE EXPEDITION over the mountains was planned for December, but when it was ready to start some of the soldiers opposed it. The year had been one of extreme drought, both in California and on the mainland, and there was a serious lack of supplies. The *Concepción* as well as the launch had failed to appear, and the safety of the settlers depended on one small vessel, which was now about to leave for Mexico. The clamors of the faint-hearted, however, merely served to bring out that optimism which was one of Kino's strongest qualities, and in his letters to the viceroy he discounts the dismal prophecies of the malcontents.

The *San José* sailed on December fourteenth, bearing Father Copart, whose stay in California was therefore short, and on that day Atondo was

THE PADRE ON HORSEBACK

at San Isidro ready to start on his expedition on the morrow, accompanied by Father Kino, twenty-nine soldiers and Indian guides, and taking eighty mules and horses. A month was spent on the exploration. They crossed the Peninsula to the South Sea in latitude twenty-six degrees, where Kino saw certain blue shells which fifteen years later became an important factor in his further movements. Meanwhile the complaints of the soldiers grew stronger, and the tide of discontent could not be stemmed even by Father Kino's optimism. A council was held, and on May 7, 1685, Atondo, his men, and the missionaries again abandoned their settlement, and their hopes for a new Christendom at San Bruno.[22]

While Kino and Captain Guzmán sailed north to look for a better site,[23] Atondo and Goñi engaged in a pearl fishing venture among the islands of the Gulf.[24] On the Sonora mainland Kino spent several days with the tribe of the Seris, who begged him to remain among them. Returning to Matanchel,[25] Atondo and Kino unexpectedly found themselves engaged in a warlike pursuit. Sent by the viceroy, they sailed in their California fleet to warn the Manila Galleon against lurking pirates, met it, and escorted it safely to Acapulco.[26] They now went to Mexico City. There, after a long delay, they learned the sad news that the conversion of the Peninsula was suspended, because of the need of funds elsewhere. Thus was the California enterprise put aside for the time being, to be revived a decade later by Kino and Salvatierra.[27]

PIMA LAND

AT THIS POINT Father Kino takes up in detail in his *Favores Celestiales*[28] the story of his career in America. As soon as he learned that the conversion of California had been suspended, he asked and obtained permission to go to the Guaymas and Seris, with whom he had dealt during his voyages from California to the mainland. Leaving Mexico City on November 20, 1686, he went to Guadalajara, where he obtained special privileges from the Audiencia. Setting forth again on December sixteenth, he reached Sonora early in 1687, and was assigned, not to the Guaymas as he had hoped, but to Pimería Alta, instead. At last he had reached the scene where his great life work was to be performed.

Pimería Alta included what is now northern Sonora and southern Arizona. It extended from the

Altar River, in Sonora, to the Gila, and from the San Pedro River to the Gulf of California and the Colorado of the West. At that day it was all included in the province of Nueva Vizcaya; later it was attached to Sonora, to which it belonged until the northern portion was cut off by the transaction called the Gadsden Purchase.

Kino found Pimería Alta occupied by different divisions of the Pima nation. Chief of these were the Pimas proper, living in the valleys of the Gila and the Salt rivers, especially in the region now occupied by the Pima Reservation. The valleys of the San Pedro and the Santa Cruz were inhabited by the Sobaipuris, now a practically extinct people, except for the strains of their blood still represented in the Pima and Papago tribes. West of the Sobaipuris, on both sides of the international boundary line, were the Papagos, or the Papabotes, as the early Spaniards called them. On the northwestern border of the region, along the lower Gila and the Colorado rivers, were the different Yuman tribes, such as the Yumas, the Cocomaricopas, the Cocopas, and the Quiquimas. All of these latter spoke the Yuman language, which was then, as it is today, quite distinct from that of the Pimas.

When Kino made his first explorations down the San Pedro and the Santa Cruz valleys, he found them each supporting ten or a dozen villages of Sobaipuris, the population of the former aggregating some two thousand persons and of the latter some two thousand five hundred. The Indians of both valleys were then practicing agriculture by irrigation and raising cotton for clothing, and maize, beans, calabashes, melons, and wheat for food. The Papagos were less advanced than the Pimas and Sobaipuris, but at Sonóita, at least, they were found practicing irrigation by means of ditches. The Yumas raised crops, but apparently without artificial irrigation. Much more notable than the acequias in use at the coming of the Spaniards, were the remains of many miles of aqueducts and the huge ruins of cities which had long before been abandoned, structures now attributed by scholars to the ancestors of the Pimas.

DOLORES

FATHER KINO arrived in Pimería Alta in March, 1687, and began without the loss of a single day a work of exploration, conversion, and mission building that lasted only one year less than a quarter of a century.[29] When he reached the scene of his labors the frontier mission station was at Cucurpe,* in the valley of the river now called San Miguel. Cucurpe still exists, a quiet little Mexican pueblo, sleeping under the shadow of the Agua Prieta Mountains, and inhabited by descendants of the Eudeve Indians who were there when Kino arrived. To the east, in Nueva Vizcaya, were the already important *reales,* or mining camps, of San Juan and Bacanuche, and to the south were numerous missions, ranches, and mining towns; but be-

---

*"En donde cantó la paloma—the place where the dove sang."

yond, in Pimería Alta, all was the unsubdued and little known country of the upper Pimas.

On the outer edge of this virgin territory, some fifteen miles above Cucurpe, on the San Miguel River, Kino founded the mission of Nuestra Señora de los Dolores (Our Lady of Sorrows), at the Indian village of Cosari. The site chosen was one of peculiar fitness and beauty. It is a commonplace to say that the missionaries always selected the most fertile spots for their missions. This is true, but it is more instructive to give the reason. They ordinarily founded their missions at or near the villages of the Indians for whom they were designed, and these were usually placed at the most fertile spots along the rich valleys of the streams.

Near where Cosari stood, the little San Miguel breaks through a narrow cañon, whose walls rise several hundred feet in height. Above and below the cañon, the river valley broadens out into rich vegas of irrigable bottom lands, half a mile or more in width and several miles in length. On the east, the valley is hemmed in by the Sierra de Santa Teresa, on the west by the Sierra del Torreón.

Closing the lower valley and hiding Cucurpe, stands Cerro Prieto; and cutting off the observer's view toward the north rises the grand and rugged Sierra Azul. At the cañon where the river breaks through, the western mesa juts out and forms a cliff approachable only from the west.

On this promontory, protected on three sides from attack, and affording a magnificent view, was placed the mission of Dolores. Here still stand its ruins, in full view of the valley above and below, of the mountain walls on the east and the west, the north and the south, and within the sound of the rushing cataract of the San Miguel as it courses through the gorge. This meager ruin on the cliff, consisting now of a mere fragment of an adobe wall and saddening piles of débris,* is the most venerable of the many mission remains in all Arizona and northern Sonora, for Our Lady of Sorrows was mother of them all, and for nearly a quarter of a century was the home of the remarkable missionary who built them.[30]

---

*This description was written in 1911. Even the wall has now disappeared, as I observed in 1932.

MISSION BUILDING

FROM HIS OUTPOST at Dolores, during the next quarter century, Kino and his companions pushed the frontier of missionary work and exploration across Pimería Alta to the Gila and Colorado rivers. By 1695 Kino had established a chain of missions up and down the Altar and the Magdalena. In April, 1700, he founded, within the present state of Arizona, the mission of San Xavier del Bac, and within the next two years those of Tumacácori and Guebavi, likewise within the present state of Arizona. Kino's exploring tours were also itinerant missions, and in the course of them he baptized and taught in numerous villages, all up and down the Gila and the lower Colorado, and in all parts of northern Pimería.

Most of these missions, after being started by

THE PADRE ON HORSEBACK

Kino, were turned over to others, or were attended by him at long range. Three of them, however, he built, nurtured, and administered personally. These temples stood in a north and south line, at Dolores, Remedios, and Cocóspora. First, last, and always Kino was a missionary. And between his long jaunts through the Pimería, his time and energy were given over to teaching his neophytes, building churches, and developing his fruitful ranches nearer home.

The story of progress in mission building occupies generous space in Kino's long reports. In these pages we can follow the church at Dolores from the day of its beginning to its completion and dedication. Kino arrived in the middle of March, 1687. Before the end of April, with the aid of the willing natives, he had built a chapel for religious services and a humble house for himself. In June Dolores already presented a busy building scene, "where with very great pleasure and with all willingness," the natives were "making . . . adobes, doors, windows, etc., for a very good house and church to replace the temporary quarters." The bells had recently arrived from Mexico. Their coming was an event; "and now," wrote Kino, "they are placed on the little church which we built during the first days. The natives are very fond of listening to their peals, never before heard in these lands. And they are very much pleased also by the pictures and other ornaments." It was six years before the new church was ready for dedication, but when that time arrived the ceremony was a holiday for all the Pimería. To it came important Spaniards, Jesuits and civilians, from all the country round. "Likewise, there came very many Pimas from the north and the west," cheering the anxious heart of the missionary, and lending a bright touch of color to the scene.

We have a precious description of Dolores which Kino wrote two years later. The establishment, under his magic management, had become temple, orchard, farm, stock ranch, and industrial plant, all combined in one. "This mission has its church adequately furnished with ornaments, chalices, ... bells, choir chapel, etc.; likewise a great many large and small cattle, oxen, fields, a garden with various kinds of garden crops, Castilian fruit trees, grapes, peaches, quinces, figs, pomegranates, pears, and apricots. It has a forge for blacksmiths, a carpenter shop, a pack train, water mill, many kinds of grain, and provisions from rich and abundant harvests of wheat and maize, besides other things, including horse and mule herds, all of which serve and are greatly needed for the house, as well as for the expeditions and new conquests and conversions, and to purchase a few gifts and attractions, with which, together with the Word of God, it is customary to contrive to win the minds and souls of the natives."

To help him manage this vast establishment Kino had built up a well-organized corps of native functionaries, civil, educational, and industrial. He continues, "likewise in ... Dolores, besides the justices, captain, governor, alcaldes, fiscal mayor, alguacil, topil ... masters of chapel and school, and mayor domos of the house, there are ... cowboys, ox-drivers, bakers, ... gardeners, and painters."

The churches at Remedios and Cocóspora were of slower growth till 1702. Then Kino turned to

THE PADRE ON HORSEBACK

completing them as a major interest. To carry on the work, he tells us, he assembled "maize, wheat, cattle, and clothing, or shop goods, such as cloth, ... blankets, and other fabrics, which are the currency that best serves in these new lands for the laborers, master carpenters, constables, military commanders, captains, and fiscales."

For beams and framework for the churches, the tireless Kino had pine timber cut and hauled from the mountains near by. To obtain the necessary tools he went personally to purchase them in the towns of Sonora. To help with the building he invited Indians from all directions, and there came, he says, "far and away more than I had requested, especially from Bac." The hills of Remedios and Cocóspora now echoed the sounds of hammer and saw. Adobes were made, walls went up, roofs were tiled. Meanwhile Kino cut a deep trail riding back and forth to supervise all this activity. "I managed all the year (1703)," he writes, "to go nearly every week through the three pueblos, looking after both spiritual and temporal things, and the building of the two new churches." That is to say, each week he

THE PADRE ON HORSEBACK

rode to Remedios, Cocóspora, and back to Dolores. The round trip was a good hundred miles.

The laborers had to be fed and clothed. During the work on these two churches, five hundred beeves and five hundred fanegas (over a thousand bushels) of wheat were eaten by the workmen. To cover their nakedness Kino spent three thousand pesos, a sum which now would be equivalent to many thousand dollars. His pack trains were all the while on the go, to and from the towns and mining camps of Sonora, carrying south pack loads of flour, maize, meat, lard, and tallow, and returning north with the precious merchandise needed for the church building.

Father Eusebio may be pardoned if he was a little vain of his two new temples. Father Leal had called Dolores the finest church in Sonora. But those of Remedios and Cocóspora were finer. "Each has a chapel of the most glorious apostle to the Indies, San Xavier," Kino tells us, "and each chapel would have cost ten thousand pesos were it not for the fertility of these new conversions."

TRAIL MAKING

KINO'S WORK as missionary was paralleled by his achievement as explorer, and to him is due the credit for the first mapping of Pimería Alta on the basis of actual exploration. The region had been entered by Fray Marcos, by Melchior Díaz, and by the main Coronado party, in the period 1539-1541. But these explorers had only passed along its eastern and western borders; for it is no longer believed that they went down the Santa Cruz. Oñate went from Moqui down the Colorado River and became acquainted with the Yumas and their neighbors, (1604–1605). Since that time settlement had edged slowly north, and the Pimas had become well known on the Sonora border. Kino tells us that before his day New Mexico traders had visited the tribe.[31] But of this contact no satisfactory information has come to us. So far as recorded history goes, therefore, the rediscovery and the detailed reconnoissance of Pimería Alta was the work of Father Kino.

Not to count the minor and unrecorded journeys among his widely separated missions, he made at least fourteen expeditions across the line into what is now Arizona. Six of them took him as far as Tumacácori, Fairbank, San Xavier del Bac, or Tucson. Six carried him to the Gila over five different routes. Twice he reached that stream by way of the Santa Cruz, returning once via Casa Grande, Sonóita, the Gulf of California, and Caborca. Once he went by way of the San Pedro, once from El Sáric across to the Gila below the Big Bend, and three times by way of Sonóita and the Camino del Diablo, along the Gila Range. Two of these expeditions carried him to Yuma and down the Colorado. Once he crossed that stream into California, and finally he reached its mouth.

East and west, between Sonóita and the eastern missions, he crossed southern Arizona several times and by various trails. In what is now Sonora he made at least half a dozen recorded journeys from Dolores to Caborca and the coast, three to the Santa Clara Mountain* to view the head of the California Gulf, and two to the coast by then unknown routes south of the Altar River. This enumeration does not include his journey to Mexico, nor the numerous other trips to distant interior points in what is now Sonora, to see the superior mission authorities, or to drive cattle and purchase supplies.

---

*Sierra del Pinacate.

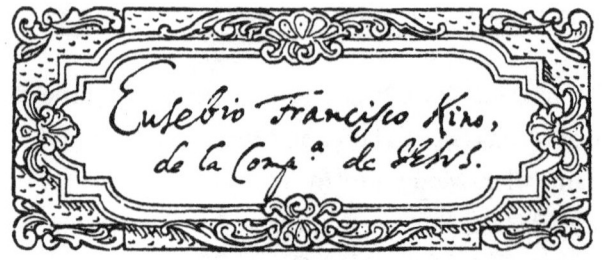

THE BLUE SHELLS

ASIDE from his search for souls in the Pimería, after 1699 Kino's most absorbing quest was made to discover a land route to California. Since the days of Cortés and Cabrillo many views had been held regarding the geography of California, some regarding it as a peninsula and others as an island. Kino had been taught by Father Aygentler, in the University of Ingolstadt, that it was a peninsula, and had come to America firm in this belief; but in deference to current opinion, and as a result of certain observations of his own, he had given up the notion, and as late as 1698 he wrote of California as "the largest island of the world." But during the journey of 1699 to the Gila occurred an incident that caused him to turn again to the peninsular theory. It was the gift, when near the Yuma junction, of certain blue shells, such as he had seen in 1685 on the Pacific coast of the Peninsula of California, and there only. If the shells had come to the Yumas from the South Sea, he reasoned, must there not be land connection with California and the ocean, by way of the Yuma country?

Kino now ceased his work on the boat he was building at Caborca and Dolores for the navigation of the Gulf, and directed his efforts to learning more about the source of the blue shells. For this purpose he made a journey in 1700 to San Xavier del Bac. Thither he called the Indians from all the villages for hundreds of miles around, and in "long talks" at night he learned that only from the South Sea could the blue shells be had.

This assurance was the inspiration of his remaining journeys. In the same year, 1700, he for the first time reached the Yuma junction, and learned that he was above the head of the Gulf, which greatly strengthened his belief in the peninsular theory. In the next year he returned to the same point by way of the Camino del Diablo, passed some distance down the Colorado, and crossed over to the

California side, towed on a raft by Indians and sitting in a basket. Finally, in 1702, his triumph came, for he again returned to the Yuma junction, descended the Colorado to the Gulf, and saw the sun rise over its head. He was now satisfied that he had demonstrated the feasibility of a land passage to California and had disproved the idea that California was an island. *"California no es isla, sino penisla,"* he now wrote in triumph. "California is not an island, but a peninsula!"

In estimating these feats of exploration we must remember the meager outfit and the limited aid with which he performed them. He was not supported and encouraged by several hundred horsemen and a great retinue of friendly Indians, as were De Soto and Coronado. On the contrary, in all but two cases he went almost unaccompanied by military aid, and more than once he went without a single white man. In one expedition, made in 1697 to the Gila, he was accompanied by Lieutenant Manje, Captain Bernal, and twenty-two soldiers. In 1701 he was escorted by Manje and ten soldiers. At other times he had no other military support than Lieutenant Manje or Captain Carrasco, without soldiers. Once Father Gilg, besides Manje, accompanied him; once two priests and two citizens. His last great exploration to the Gila was made with only one other white man in his party, while in 1694, 1700, and 1701 he reached the Gila with no living soul save his Indian servants. But he was usually well supplied with horses and mules from his own ranches, for he took at different times as many as fifty, sixty, eighty, ninety, one hundred and five, and even one hundred and thirty head, part of them to serve as relay, and part to be left at some Indian village, to become a nucleus for a new ranch to support some new mission of which he was dreaming.

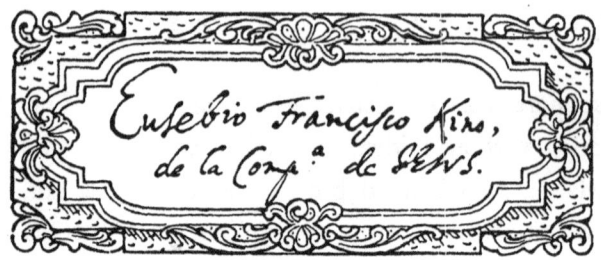

CATTLE KING

THE WORK which Father Kino did as ranchman, or stockman, would alone stamp him as an unusual business man and make him worthy of remembrance. He was easily the cattle king of his day and region. From the small outfit supplied him from the older missions to the east and south, within fifteen years he established the beginnings of ranching in the valleys of the Magdalena, the Altar, the Santa Cruz, the San Pedro, and the Sonóita. The stock-raising industry of nearly twenty places on the modern map owes its beginnings on a considerable scale to this indefatigable man. And it must not be supposed that he did this for private gain, for he did not own a single animal. It was to furnish a food supply for the Indians of the missions established and to be established, and to give these missions a basis of economic prosperity and independence. It would be impossible to give a detailed statement of his work of this nature, but some of the exact facts are necessary to convey the impression. Most of the data, of course, were unrecorded, but from those available it is learned that stock ranches were established by him or directly under his supervision at Dolores, Caborca, Tubutama, San Ignacio, Imuris, Magdalena, Quiburi, Tumacácori, Cocóspora, San Xavier del Bac, Bacoancos, Guebavi, Síboda, Búsanic, Sonóita, San Lázaro, Sáric, Santa Bárbara, and Santa Eulalia.

Characteristic of Kino's economic efforts are those reflected in Father Saeta's letter thanking him for the present of one hundred and fifteen head of cattle and as many sheep for the beginnings of a ranch at Caborca. In 1699 a ranch was established at Sonóita for the triple purpose of supplying the little mission there, furnishing food for the missionaries of California, if perchance they should reach that point, and as a base of supplies for the explorations which Kino hoped to undertake and did undertake to the Yumas and Cocomaricopas, of whom he had heard while on the Gila. In 1700, when the mission of San Xavier was founded, Kino rounded up the fourteen hundred head of cattle on the ranch of his own mission of Dolores, divided them into two equal droves, and sent one of them under his Indian overseer to Bac, where the necessary corrals were constructed.

Not only his own missions, but those of sterile California must be supplied; and in the year 1700 Kino took from his own ranches seven hundred cattle and sent them to Salvatierra, across the Gulf, at Loreto, a transaction similar to several others that are recorded.

And it must not be forgotten that Kino conducted this cattle industry with Indian labor, almost without the aid of a single white man. An illustration of his method and of his difficulties is found in the fact that the important ranch at Tumacácori, Arizona, was founded with cattle and sheep driven at Kino's orders one hundred miles across the country from Caborca by the very Indians who had murdered Father Saeta. There was always the danger that the mission Indians would revolt and run off the stock, as they did in 1695; and the danger, more imminent, that the hostile Apaches, Janos, and Jocomes would do this damage and add to it the destruction of human life.

PROTECTOR OF THE BORDER

To THE PIMAS, Kino was the Great White Father. They loved him, he loved them, and they were ready to die for each other. To him they flocked as if drawn by a magnet. From northeast, north, northwest, and west they beat trails to the door of the missionary wizard. Chiefs and warriors went to attend councils; to take part in church fiestas; to be baptized; to assist in planting, harvesting, and roundups. They had a childish desire to satisfy Kino's every wish. He showed an interest in blue shells. Thereafter delegation after delegation trudged from the far distant Colorado bearing presents of shells in such number that Kino's mission must have resembled a museum of conchology.

Kino's almost hypnotic influence over the Pimas gave him the position of protector of the Sonora frontier. When they heard that he had been ordered back to California (1697), citizens and soldiers protested, declaring that in the defence of the border he was worth more than a garrison. Sonora was pestered by Indian ravages. Year after year the Apaches, Jocomes, Sumas, and Mansos made incursions into the Spanish settlements. The Apache loved the taste of horse flesh and he knew where to get it. Cattle, sheep, and goats were not beneath his notice. Sonora was a ranching country and there the Apaches levied tribute. All too frequently their forays were attended by cold blooded murder of peaceful citizens.

Sometimes Sonorans attributed these outrages to the Pimas. But whoever did so had a fight on his hands. Any such charge Kino resented with all his fervent spirit, and with the full force of his ever ready pen. The falsity of the accusation was generally patent, for the Apaches were quite as hostile to Pimas as to Spaniards, and year after year they beat against the easternmost Pima settlements in San Pedro Valley.

The Pimas were valiant fighters, and every blow

THE PADRE ON HORSEBACK

they struck for themselves was a blow for the Spaniards as well. On this help, after Kino arrived, the Sonorans came to rely. The soldiers, when they organized a campaign against the Apaches, would call for a levy of Pimas. To raise the Indian forces they depended on Kino. Promptly he would send runners to the villages to notify the chiefs, naming place and date of the rendezvous. And his services did not end here. On such occasions it was customary for him to furnish beeves for Indians and even for soldiers during the campaign.

Head of the eastern Sobaipuris, and Kino's main reliance, was Chief Coro—so-called because his resonant voice was equal to a whole chorus. More than once Capitán Coro led his braves against the Apaches; more than once he stemmed an Apache invasion into Pimería. Every such example was seized upon by Kino as proof of Pima loyalty and of the falsity of charges against them.

A single illustration, related by Kino, will suffice. One March day in 1698 the Apaches came down in full force on Quiburi.* With unwonted humanity

---
*Near the site of Fairbank.

the opposing chiefs agreed to fight the battle by champions, ten on a side. Capotcari headed the Apache ten; Coro led the Pima phalanx. In shooting, the opponents were about equal, but in parrying arrows with their shields the Pimas were the more dexterous. After a terrific struggle nine of the Apaches were stretched out on the ground. Then Capotcari fell and his head was pounded to a jelly with stones. The Apache mob—several hundred in number—now took to flight, with Coro and his Pimas in full pursuit. It was a grand rout. For leagues the ground was strewn with the Apache dead and dying; women and children were captured and enslaved.

Coro had won a great victory. He must send the news to Father Kino. Soon a runner was on his way over the hills to Dolores, carrying a long notched stick, each notch standing for a dead Apache. Kino in turn hurried messengers to the Sonora settlements to spread the tidings.

But there were doubters. The story was exaggerated, they said. The allies could not win such a victory. This was a challenge to the champion of the Pimas. Forthwith he saddled his best horse, took a companion, rode northeast a hundred and more miles to the battlefield, and with qualified witnesses counted the Apache cadavers scattered through the wilderness. "We saw and counted fifty-four corpses near by," says Kino, "thirty-one of men and twenty-three of women. The natives gave us various spoils, which we brought away with us, among them an arquebus, powder, and balls, a leathern jacket, buffalo and deer skins, bows and arrows, and scalps of the above-mentioned enemies."

This was gruesome business, but Kino's Pimas were vindicated. The news spread. In the Sonora settlements church bells rang with jubilation, and Kino was showered with letters of congratulation. Coro and his brave bowmen received the promised reward, but Kino was the hero of the occasion.

HARD RIDING

KINO'S ENDURANCE in the saddle was worthy of a seasoned cowboy. This is evident from the bare facts with respect to the long journeys which he made. When he went to the City of Mexico in the fall of 1695, being then past the age of fifty, he made the journey in fifty-three days, between November sixteenth and January eighth. The distance, via Guadalajara, is no less than fifteen hundred miles, making his average, not counting the stops which he made at Guadalajara and other important places, nearly thirty miles per day. In November, 1697, when he went to the Gila, he rode about seven hundred or eight hundred miles in thirty days, not counting out the stops. On his journey in 1698 to the Gila he made an average of twenty-five or more miles a day for twenty-six days, over an unknown country. In 1699 he made the trip to and from the lower Gila, about eight or nine hundred miles, in thirty-five days, an average of ten leagues a day, or twenty-five to thirty miles. In October and November, 1699, he rode two hundred and forty leagues in thirty-nine days. In September and October, 1700, he rode three hundred and eighty-four leagues, or perhaps one thousand miles, in twenty-six days. This was an average of nearly forty miles a day. In 1701, he made over four hundred leagues or more than eleven hundred miles, in thirty-five days, an average of over thirty miles a day. No, these figures are not fanciful; they are taken from his actual diaries!

Thus we see that it was customary for Kino to make an average of thirty or more miles a day for weeks or months at a time, when he was on these missionary tours, and out of this time are to be counted the long stops which he made to preach to and baptize the Indians and to say Mass.

A special instance of his hard riding is found in the journey which he made in November, 1699, with Father Leal, the Visitor of the missions. After twelve days of continuous travel, supervising, baptizing, and preaching up and down the Santa Cruz Valley, going the while at the average rate of twenty-three miles (nine leagues) a day, he left Father Leal at Batki to go home by carriage over a more direct route, while he and Manje sped "á la ligera" to the west and northwest, to see if there were any sick Indians to baptize. Going thirteen leagues (thirty-three miles) on the eighth, he baptized two infants and two adults at the village of San Rafael. On the ninth he rode nine leagues to another village, made a census of four hundred Indians, preached to them, and continued sixteen more leagues to another village, making nearly sixty miles for the day. On the tenth he made a census of the assembled throng of three hundred persons, preached, baptized three sick persons, distributed presents, and then rode thirty-three leagues (some seventy-five miles) over a pass in the mountains to Sonóita, arriving there in the night, having stopped to make a census of, preach to, and baptize in two villages on the way. After four hours of sleep on the eleventh, he baptized and preached, and then rode, that day and night, the fifty leagues (or one hundred to one hundred and twenty-five miles) that lie between Sonóita and Búsanic, where he overtook Father Leal. During the last three days he had ridden no less than one hundred and eight leagues, or from two hundred and fifty to three hundred miles, counting, preaching to, and baptizing in five villages on the way. And yet he was up the next morning, preaching, baptizing, and supervising the butchering of cattle for supplies. Truly this was strenuous work for a man of fifty-five.

Another instance of his disregard of toil in ministering to others may be cited. On the morning of May 3, 1700, he was at Tumacácori, on his way to Dolores, from the founding of Mission San Xavier del Bac. As he was about to say Mass at sunrise, he received an urgent message from Father Campos, begging him to hasten to San Ignacio to help save a poor Indian whom the soldiers had imprisoned and were about to execute on the following day. Stopping to say Mass and to write a hurried letter to Captain Escalante, he rode by midnight to

THE PADRE ON HORSEBACK

Imuris, and arrived at San Ignacio in time to say early Mass and to save the Indian from death. The direct route by rail from Tumacácori to Imuris is sixty-two miles, and to San Ignacio it is seventy. If Kino went the then usual route by the Santa Cruz River, he must have ridden seventy-five or more miles on this errand of mercy in considerably less than a day.

STRONG OF HEART

KINO'S PHYSICAL COURAGE is attested by his whole career in America, spent in exploring unknown wilds and laboring among untamed savages. But it is especially shown by several particular episodes in his life. In March and April, 1695, the Pimas of the Altar Valley rose in revolt. At Caborca Father Saeta was killed and became the protomartyr of Pimería Alta. At Caborca and Tubutama seven servants of the missions were slain, and at Caborca, Tubutama, Imuris, San Ignacio and Magdalena—the whole length of the Altar and Magdalena valleys—the mission churches and other buildings were burned and the stock killed or stampeded. The missionary of Tubutama fled over the mountains to Cucurpe. San Ignacio being attacked by three hundred warriors, Father Campos fled to the

THE PADRE ON HORSEBACK

same refuge, guarded on each side by two soldiers. At Dolores Father Kino, Lieutenant Manje, and three citizens of Bacanuche awaited the onslaught. An Indian who had been stationed on the mountains, seeing the smoke at San Ignacio, fled to Dolores with the story that Father Campos and all the soldiers had been killed. Manje sped to Opodepe to get aid; the three citizens hurried home to Bacanuche, and Kino was left alone. When Manje returned next day, together they hid the treasures of the church in a cave, but in spite of the soldiers' entreaties that they should flee, Kino insisted on returning to the mission to await death, which they did. Fortunately they were not killed. It is indicative of the modesty of this great soul that in his own history this incident in his life is passed over in complete silence. But Manje, who was weak or wise enough to wish to flee, was also generous and brave enough to record the padre's heroism and his own fears.

In 1701 Kino made his first exploration down the Colorado below the Yuma junction—the first that had been made for almost a century. With him was one Spaniard, the only other white man in the party. As they left the Yuma country and entered that of the Quiquimas, the Spaniard, Kino tells us in his diary, "on seeing such a great number of new people," and such people—that is, they were giants in size—became frightened and fled, and was seen no more. But the missionary, thus deserted, instead of turning back, dispatched messages that he was safe, continued down the river two days, and crossed the Colorado, guided by tall Yumas of awe-inspiring mien, into territory never trod by white men since 1540. Perhaps he was in no danger, but the situation had proved too much for the nerve of his white companion, at least.

VELARDE'S EULOGY

AND WHAT KIND of a man personally was Father Kino to those who knew him intimately? Was he rugged, coarse fibered, and adapted by nature to such a rough frontier life of exposure? I know of no portrait of him made by sunlight or the brush, but there is, fortunately, a picture drawn by the pen of his companion during the last eight years of his life, and his successor at Dolores. Father Luís Velarde tells us that Kino was a modest, humble, gentle ascetic, of medieval type, drilled by his religious training to complete self-effacement. I should not be surprised to find that, like Father Junípero Serra, he was slight of body as he was gentle of mind. Velarde says of him:

"Permit me to add what I observed in the eight years during which I was his companion. His conversation was of the mellifluous names of Jesus and Mary, and of the heathen for whom he was ever offering prayers to God. In saying his breviary he always wept. He was edified by the lives of the saints, whose virtues he preached to us. When he publicly reprimanded a sinner he was choleric. But if anyone showed him personal disrespect he controlled his temper to such an extent that he made it a habit to exalt whomsoever mistreated him by word, deed, or in writing.... And if it was to his face that they were said, he embraced the one who spoke them, saying, 'You are and ever will be my dearest master!' even though he did not like him. And then, perhaps, he would go and lay the insults at the feet of the Divine Master and the sorrowing Mother, into whose temple he went to pray a hundred times a day.[32]

"After supper, when he saw us already in bed, he would enter the church, and even though I sat up the whole night reading, I never heard him come out to get the sleep of which he was very sparing. One night I casually saw someone whipping him mercilessly [as a means of penance]. He always took his food without salt, and with mixtures of herbs which made it more distasteful. No one ever saw in him any vice whatsoever, for the discovery of lands and the conversion of souls had purified him.

"These, then, are the virtues of Father Kino: he prayed much, and was considered as without vice. He neither smoked nor took snuff, nor wine, nor slept in a bed. He was so austere that he never used wine except to celebrate Mass, nor had any other bed than the sweat blankets of his horse for a mattress, and two Indian blankets [for a cover]. He never had more than two coarse shirts, because he gave everything as alms to the Indians. He was merciful to others, but cruel to himself. While violent fevers were lacerating his body, he tried no remedy for six days except to get up to celebrate Mass and to go to bed again. And by thus weakening and dismaying Nature he conquered the fevers."

Is there any wonder that such a man as this could endure the hardships of exploration?

Kino died at the age of sixty-six, at Magdalena, one of the missions he had founded. His companion when the end came was Father Agustín de

Campos, for eighteen years his colaborer. Velarde thus describes his last moments:

"Father Kino died in the year 1711, having spent twenty-four years in glorious labors in this Pimería, which he entirely covered in forty expeditions, made as best they could be made by two or three zealous workers. When he died he was almost seventy years old. He died as he had lived, with extreme humility and poverty. In token of this, during his last illness he did not undress. His deathbed, as his bed had always been, consisted of two calfskins for a mattress, two blankets such as the Indians use for covers, and a pack-saddle for a pillow. Nor did the entreaties of Father Agustín move him to anything else. He died in the house of the Father where he had gone to dedicate a finely made chapel in his pueblo of Santa Magdalena, consecrated to San Francisco Xavier.[33] . . . When he was singing the Mass of the dedication he felt indisposed, and it seems that the Holy Apostle, to whom he was ever devoted, was calling him, in order that, being buried in his chapel, he might accompany him, as we believe, in glory."

THE PADRE ON HORSEBACK

The words of that eloquent writer, John Fiske, in reference to Las Casas, Protector of the Indians, are not inapplicable to Father Kino. He says:

"In contemplating such a life, all words of eulogy seem weak and frivolous. The historian can only bow in reverent awe before ... [such] a figure. When now and then in the course of centuries God's providence brings such a life into this world, the memory of it must be cherished by mankind as one of its most precious and sacred possessions. For the thoughts, the words, the deeds of such a man, there is no death. The sphere of their influence goes on widening forever. They bud, they blossom, they bear fruit, from age to age."

NOTES

¹ Sommervogel, *Bibliothèque de la Compagnie de Jesus, première partie,* vol. iv, 1044; Clavigero, *Historia de la Baja California,* 39; Beristáin, *Biblioteca Hispano-Americana,* 1819. Bancroft, *North Mexican States and Texas* (vol. i, 250, footnote).

² Sommervogel, *ibid.,* vol. iv, 1044; Stöcklein, *Der Neue Welt–Bott mit allerhand Nachrichten dern Missionariorum Soc. Jesu,* erster band (Augsburg and Grätz, 1726).

³ Bolton, H. E., *Kino's Historical Memoir of Pimería Alta,* I, 96–97.

⁴ "Brief P. Adami Gerstl, S.J., an seinem Vatter," Puebla, July 14, 1681, in Stöcklein, *Neue Welt–Bott,* Theil i, num. 31.

⁵ An account of the wreck and of the journey of some of the Fathers to America is given in "Brief Patris Mancker" Mexico, January 25, 1681, in Stöcklein, *Neue Welt–Bott,* Theil i, num. 30, pp. 85–90.

⁶ Beristáin, *Biblioteca Hispano–Americana Septentrional, Adiciones y Correcciones* (1898), pp. 392–393. Gerstl says that the voyage lasted ninety-six days, beginning January 29. Counting to May 3 would give only ninety-five days.

⁷ See Stöcklein, "Vorrede des ersten Theils," and missionary letters by Borango (num. 2) Tilpe (num. 3, 64), Strobach (num. 4, num. 5), Cuculinus (num. 7, num. 8), Garzia and Bonani (num. 9), Mancker (num. 12, num. 20), Ratkay (num. 28, num. 29), Gerstl (num. 31), Neuman (num. 32), Gilg (num. 33, num. 35), Klein (num. 37).

⁸ *Exposicion Astronomica de el Cometa, que el Año de 1680, por los meses de Noviembre, y Diziembre, y este Año*

de 1681, por los Meses de Enero y Febrero, se ha visto en todo el mundo, y le ha observado en la Ciudad de Cadiz, El P. Eusebio Francisco Kino de la Compañia de Jesus. Con licencia, en Mexico por Francisco Rodríguez Lupercio, 1681, 4° ffnc. 28, 1 carte. This title is taken from Sommervogel [*Bibliothèque,* vol. iv., 1044] who gives also the circumstances of the composition of the work. Bancroft gives the first word of the title as "Explicación" [*North Mexican States and Texas,* vol. i, 251], while Beristáin gives several other variations from the above form. The title alone proves that Kino arrived in Mexico in 1681. He saw the comet in Cádiz between November, 1680, and February, 1681, and by implication, only in Cádiz; therefore he could not have reached Mexico while the comet was still visible. For the impression made by Kino on the viceroy, see the letter by Father Neuman, from Sisokitschik, Nueva Vizcaya, July 29, 1686, in *Neue Welt–Bott,* Theil i, 106.

[9] Venegas, *Noticia,* vol. i, 219; *Autos sobre los Parages que ha descubierto en las Yslas Californias el Almirante don Ysidro de Atondo,* in *El Virey de la Nueva España da cuenta,* etc., A.G.I., 1–1–2/31.

[10] Venegas, *Noticia,* vol. i, 219, conveys the impression that the royal *cédula* of December 29, 1679, named Kino cosmographer, but he is not mentioned in that document [*Baja, California Cédulas,* Ms., Bancroft Library, 74]. The selection of the missionaries was made by the Provincial, Father Pardo [Alegre, *Hist.,* vol. iii, 42–43]. See also Clavigero, 36; *Documentos para la Historia de Mexico,* cuarta série, vol. v, 11–12; Bancroft, *North Mexican States,* vol. i, 186–187.

[11] These movements of Father Kino between his arrival in Mexico and his departure for California are revealed by a manuscript *expediente* entitled *Sobre pertenencia del Govierno Espiritual de Californias*, A.G.I., 67-4-2.

[12] *Expediente sobre pertenencia;* Alegre, *Hiſt.*, vol. iii, 27-28.

[13] His application was made at Pueblo de Nio, March 25, 1682. *Expediente sobre pertenencia.*

[14] Bancroft [*North Mexican States*, vol. i, 187] states that Father Goñi did not go with this expedition. This is a mistake, it being Father Copart and not Father Goñi who went later.

[15] March 18.

[16] "A Descent made by the Spaniards, in the Island of California," in Lockman, *Travels of the Jesuits*, vol. i, 408-420. For other forms of this narrative see Bancroft, *North Mexican States*, vol. i, 187, footnote 24. Some doubt was expressed as to whether or not this was the old Bay of La Paz (*ibid.*, 410). It was at any rate clearly the one now so-called.

[17] The formal act of possession by Atondo is preserved for us in Alegre, *Hiſt.*, vol. iii, 43-45; that by Kino and Goñi is contained in *Expediente Sobre pertenencia.*

[18] Venegas, *Noticia*, vol. i, 222-230; *Autos sobre los Parages.*

[19] *Tercera Entrada en 21 de Diciembre de 1683* (printed in *Documentos para la Hiſtoria de Mexico*, cuarta série, vol. i, 405-458). Original manuscript in the archives of Mexico. The details are in *Autos sobre los Parages.*

[20] On the other hand he showed little interest in the tribal customs, which so engaged the attention of many missionaries.

[21] *North Mexican States*, vol. i, 251. Bancroft's whole treatment of the subject here is hazy and inaccurate. Kino returned with Andrés on September 25.

[22] For the above events see *Autos sobre los Parages*.

[23] The story of this voyage is recorded in Guzmán's diary.

[24] Father Goñi to the Bishop of Guadalajara, on board the bilander, at San Ignacio, September 22, 1685, manuscript in No. 30. Venegas [*Noticia*, vol. i, 236] makes it appear that the settlement of San Bruno was removed by Atondo during this voyage, but from the contemporary correspondence it is clear that this is a mistake. It had already been abandoned in May.

[25] On the way they stopped at San Bruno.

[26] Father Kino to the Bishop of Guadalajara, Colegio de Guadalajara, October 10, 1685. Kino to the Bishop of Guadalajara, Matanchel, November 15, 1685. Kino to the Bishop of Guadalajara, Compostela, November 5, 1685, in *No. 30. El Obispo da quenta*.

[27] Kino to the Bishop of Guadalajara, Casa Profesa, February 15, 1686; Venegas, *Noticia*, vol. i, 236–240; *real cédula*, December 22, 1685, A.G.I. 67-3-28. Transcript in Bancroft Library. According to a dispatch from the Audiencia of Guadalajara, April 27, 1702, the abandonment of California cost Father Copart his reason, which at that date he had not recovered. A.G.I. 67-3-28. Transcript in Bancroft Library.

[28] Since this section is based largely on the *Favores Celestiales*, numerous specific references will not be given.

[29] It may be of interest to note that Kino arrived in Pimería Alta in the very month of La Salle's assassination in the wilds of Texas.

[30] The ruins of the Mission of Dolores are on Rancho de Dolores, on the hill directly overlooking the residence of the owner. They were visited by the writer in 1911, and again in 1932.

[31] Father Kino is authority for the statement that before his day the Spaniards of New Mexico had traded with the Sobaipuris of the San Pedro Valley.

[32] The allusion is to the name of the mission, Nuestra Señora de los Dolores.

[33] I have seen no confirmation of Father Benz's story that Kino was killed by rebel Indians. From what is said here it seems altogether improbable. The original certificate of Kino's burial agrees with what is said here. See *Catholic Encyclopedia,* vol. viii, 660.

*Here
endeth the sketch
of Eusebio Francisco Kino,
"The Padre on Horseback," superb
missionary, church builder, explorer and ranchman.
This first edition was designed by Signor Sivertson and printed
by Marcus Brower & Company, San Francisco
in the month of September, nineteen
hundred and thirty-two.
The drawings are by
William Wilke*

✶

www.ingramcontent.com/pod-product-compliance
Lightning Source LLC
Chambersburg PA
CBHW031408040426
42444CB00005B/474